YOUR KNOWLEDGE HAS VALUE

- We will publish your bachelor's and master's thesis, essays and papers

- Your own eBook and book - sold worldwide in all relevant shops

- Earn money with each sale

Upload your text at www.GRIN.com
and publish for free

Bibliographic information published by the German National Library:

The German National Library lists this publication in the National Bibliography; detailed bibliographic data are available on the Internet at http://dnb.dnb.de .

This book is copyright material and must not be copied, reproduced, transferred, distributed, leased, licensed or publicly performed or used in any way except as specifically permitted in writing by the publishers, as allowed under the terms and conditions under which it was purchased or as strictly permitted by applicable copyright law. Any unauthorized distribution or use of this text may be a direct infringement of the author s and publisher s rights and those responsible may be liable in law accordingly.

Imprint:

Copyright © 2018 GRIN Verlag
Print and binding: Books on Demand GmbH, Norderstedt Germany
ISBN: 9783668735484

This book at GRIN:

https://www.grin.com/document/430701

Caroline Mutuku

Significance of understanding Human Resource Management from the Diversity Perspective

GRIN Verlag

GRIN - Your knowledge has value

Since its foundation in 1998, GRIN has specialized in publishing academic texts by students, college teachers and other academics as e-book and printed book. The website www.grin.com is an ideal platform for presenting term papers, final papers, scientific essays, dissertations and specialist books.

Visit us on the internet:

http://www.grin.com/

http://www.facebook.com/grincom

http://www.twitter.com/grin_com

Significance of understanding Human Resource Management from the Diversity Perspective

For more than a hundred years, human resource management, as a practice and discipline in people management in an organization, has evolved in definition and in scope. The most popular definition of human resource management is that provided by Storey and Armstrong. The duo define human resource management as "a distinctive approach to employment management seeking to accomplish competitive advantage through strategic deployment of highly capable and committed labour using an integrated array of cultural, structural and personnel technique" (Itika 2011, p. 12). Human resource management can further be defined as a management practice and a strategic approach towards employee management in ways that would result in attainment of organizational goals, objectives and mission. According to these definitions, human resource management uses tools that attracts, motivates, develops and retains the effective function of the management of people. His may not be easy as people are workplaces are made up of several differences that are visible or invisible, through age, marital status, gender, sexual orientation, ethnicity, religion, personality and culture amongst others. Diversity in workplaces has resulted in the discriminations of certain individuals (OECD 2012). For instance, gender inequality is vice that cut across the globe, religion and ethnic segregation separates individuals in Middle East workplaces. In China, rural migrants are looked down upon by the urbanites and are mistreated in whatever kind of jobs they are allocated. Xenophobic incidences have widely been reported in South African workplaces, while the United States is blamed for racial discrimination.

A diverse workforce is made up of several beliefs, values, perspectives in world-viewing, understanding and any other unique formation. The escalation of internationalization and globalization at workplaces has promoted the need to understand human resource management in terms of diversity (OECD 2012). Although there is great understanding of how diversity impacts of the achievement of organizational goals, there are still multi-national corporations that are hesitant in hiring and promoting ethnic minorities and female employees, particularly to senior management positions. There have been studies that have shown that although certain human resource management practices are meant to increase diversity at workplaces, they have failed in highlighting the increase in top management. For instance, planning for training fails to lead to the top management diversity and the overall organizational diversity. Moreover, organizations made up of diverse workforces do not remunerate well their labour (OECD 2012).

Still, there is need for understanding human resource management in the perspective of diversity. A diverse conscious management comes up with innovative concepts and solutions to organizational challenges. A diversity-based human resource management results in information sharing that benefit in bottom-line outcomes (Onday 2016). Therefore, the management of diversity should be founded on diversity recognition and the differences occurring within the workforce instead of viewing it as an issue that need to be resolved. A diverse workforce brainstorms better, and exhibits corporate behaviours linked to increasing the efficiency of the organization. Therefore, human resource management based upon value diversity is one of the best sources of competitive advantage. Nonetheless, the probable benefits of diversity at workplaces are not only achieved through having a diverse workforce alone (European Commission 2012). The competency of human resource management in its management counts better in attaining the value associated with diversity, more particular in the today's flexible, collaborative non-hierarchical management. Human resource managers, therefore, need not only understand that individuals at their workplaces are different, but, as well establish atmosphere that mines out the value of diversity (Onday 2016).

The core to the management of diversity at workplaces is based through the development and the implementation of people-centred policies. Diversity management is a concept revolving around employees human resource management functions as the custodian to these people management processes with functions undertaken in diversity management overlapping into those undertaken in by human resource management (Shen et al., 2009, p. 235). With the definition of human resource management as a practice assisting in issues in labour management by lining the workers or individuals involved in the production of organizational goods and services, human resource management matters in the acquisition of services from diverse people, developing their skills and motivating them to perform exceedingly high (Doaei & Najminia n.d.).

The functions of human resource management indicate that the practices are significant in enhancing the performance of an organization which is also the aim of diversity management (Onday 2016). This only occurs when the right people from whatever diverse differences are attracted, identified and retained with the skills, ability and knowledge required for the jobs. Human resource management in turn gets the workforce to behave in ways that support the achievement of organizational goals and not in the ways that diverse values held by individual workers conflict. Therefore, it is significant for an organization to employ human resource management practices that utilizes valued resources held by its diverse workforce (Burma 2014).

Understanding human resource management through diversity helps in understanding individual differences, and in the equitable development of each and every member of the workplace. An application human resource management tools while addressing inequality in recruitment, training, appraisal, promotion and reward enhance inclusiveness, equal employment opportunities and promote innovativeness in a diverse workforce. Human resource management practices are critical in overcoming group or individual process issues while it improves on the triple bottom line. Effective human resource strategies are geared towards organizational flexibility, knowledge creation, learning and establishment of an environment conducive to the management of diversity. Therefore, it is clear that management of diversity is a critical part in human resource management (Shen et al. 2009).Clearly, there is no organization across the world that can be a going concern without valuing workforce diversity (Bedi 2014).

Among the diversity observed at workplaces are gender differences. Gender asymmetries and characteristics of workplace structures founded on patriarchal concepts do not permit an organization in attaining its full potential. Gender aspect in human resource management is among the major issues in developed countries that are addressed at local and national levels. This may be due to the growth in the number of female employees in these countries. Despite the efforts to have human resource management understood in the context of gender, the occupational patterns of women and men differ greatly. For instance, the growth in the female workforce in the part-time jobs provides a significant tendency (Standing, 1999, p. 2). It is argued that by providing part-time jobs to the female workforce, women are permitted to maintain the work-life balance. In addition, companies providing flexible time to their female workforce are among those commended in the accomplishment in assessing human resource management through a gender lens (Senyucel 2009).

Workplace gender asymmetry is linked to legal designed stereotypic socio-economic relations as well as stereotypes in the division of labour across genders. For instance, in traditional gender attitudes, the biological nature of women impact on their professional success. Organizations applying these stereotypes would argue that female labour is much more expensive than male labour. In addition, management practices basing their decision on the argument that the psychological characteristics of women limit their capacity at workplaces fail to achieve their goals. Human resource managers must understand that such stereotypes bar the full development and realization of women potential in the labour market, thus hinders the attainment of organization goals (Standing 1999).

Labour activities in the 1980s and early months of 1990s resulted to the destruction of most of gender-based stereotypes in the workplaces. The introduction of private property rights across the global, for instance, led to the collapse of social ideological frameworks that stereotyped women from doing what were thoughts to jobs belonging to men. The process led o even more destruction at workplaces and its role in the society. Consequently, women became objectionable competitors to men in the labour market. Statistics mentioned by Kosheleva and Zavyalova (2011, p.3) indicates that the average economic activities attributed the female workforces is 63% compared to 72% of the male colleagues. Women in Denmark, Norway and Sweden have higher indicator than the global one. This is an indication that the employment structure of women has undergone a rigorous transformation, thanks to gender-based human resource management. Initially, women were thrown out of competitive sectors into low-paid and low-skilled areas that were coupled with high risks. However, with the reforms in human resource management women began undertaking entrepreneurial activities (Kosheleva & Zavyalova 2011).

From the above discussion, understanding of human resource management in the perspective of gender is significant in assessing the manner in which equal opportunities concepts are operationalized. Moreover it aids in evaluating on how different human resource management initiatives are used in the promotion of gender equality at workplaces (Davies & Thomas 2011). Gender-based human resource management assessment provides the manner in which managers consider different genders as candidates of different roles and responsibilities. For instance, traditional human resource practices provide that managers would not consider women for positions such as loaders, installers, security guards, drillers amongst others. Similarly, there are organizations that do not employ men in jobs considered to be female ones. These jobs include cloakroom attendant, janitor, office manager, secretary and accountants. Significantly, such moves affect the manner in which human resource managers pay and dismiss their workforce. For instance, statistics indicate that men are given more pay compared to their male counterparts. Men are paid up to 30% more than women who have similar qualifications and quantity of job done (Kosheleva & Zavyalova 2011).

The significance of gender awareness in human resource management is due to the understanding of importance of gender in the people positioning at workplaces. Gender conscious human resource management practices recognize that gender impacts on career patterns, occupational choices, and work practices. It is, thus, significant to note that there is practical need in the consideration for the relationship between the compositions of gender in organizational workforce. In addition, it impacts on the type of recruitment strategy, conditions, contracts, and terms that are geared towards making an effective human resources in the organization.

Gender-based human resource management as well aids in the provision of affirmative actions to women who have been for a long-time historically misrepresented at workplaces. This is the context of the small number of women in the management levels and in the policy roles together with the lack of female voices as industrial stakeholders. The gendered nature of human resource management is significant in the attainment of organizational goals through an increased utilization of human resources (Standing 1999).

Across the globe, there are clear preferences in the manner in which labour is remunerated across genders. Female workers prefer having their pay fixed across the year or for the job done. This preference is different to what man want. The male workforce prefers having their pay calculated as per the result of their jobs. The preference indicates abroad-spread of likings with women preferring a more stable form of income (Kosheleva & Zavyalova 2011).

Gender-based human resource management evaluation also determines the manner in which employees of different genders are treated in dismissal (Senyucel 2009). Although a large number of managers do no care on gender while dismissing their workforce, the number of those who would go for a female worker to a male worker when forced to choose on one individual are significantly high. Nonetheless, gender is a mere factor in the evaluation of employees. This is similar to the absence of gender factor in work evaluation in jobs that are done by both genders. There is insignificant difference in the requirement to both female and male workers. However, differences in the requirement in the selection of employees are argued to be an increase in the demand for men than for women at workplaces (Kosheleva & Zavyalova 2011). Therefore, understanding of human resource management from a gendered based perspective highlights the inequality between women and men in the development of the requisite knowledge and skills. It also shows on how pays are fairly distributed and the workforce equally treated and assisted across genders towards the advancement of the career of an employee (Intrahealth 2015). The occurrence of gender discrimination and inequality at workplaces outside the awareness of human resource management policy makers leads to attrition, work absenteeism, higher employee turnover and even poor health and lack of morale among the employees. This results in having low-skilled or under-qualified employees in attaining the organizational goals. Therefore, human resource management policies that attend to the equality of the genders fully accomplish organizational labour coverage and goals. Moreover, organizations that view human resource diversely improve on their effectiveness and organizational outcomes (Kosheleva & Zavyalova 2011).

There is need for human resource managers to understand that inequality at workplaces on the basis of gender is core barrier for the entry, retention and re-entry of paid skilled workers. Therefore, there is need for organizations to identify patterns that would guide its workforce, policy, planning, management and development (Intrahealth 2015). Moreover, gender conscious human resource management aids in coming up with policies and practices that assists in the elimination of gender discrimination and inequality. Such policies and practices helps in the mitigation for the advancement of women at workplaces and attainment of organizational goals. Moreover, gender-based human resource management gives attention to cultural practices that impact on the entry and exit of female workers like events such as pregnancy and childcare that may impact on the attraction, and retention of female workers.

References

Bedi, P. 2014, Workforce Diversity Management, *IOSR Journal of Business and Management*, vol. 16, no. 4, pp. 102-107.

Burma, Z. 2014, Human Resource Management and its Application in Today's organizations, *International Journal of Education and Social Science*, vol. 1, no. 2, pp. 85-94.

Doaei, H & Najminia, R. n.d, How Far Does HRM Differ from PM. *European Scientific Journal*, vol. 8, no. 13, pp. 161-171.

European Commission 2012, *Managing Diversity at Work*, Luxemburg: European Commission Justice.

Intrahealth 2015, Gender Equality in Human Resources for Health: What Does this Mean and What Can we Do?, *IntraHealth International*.

Itika, J 2011, *Fundamentals of Human resource Management: Emerging Experiences from Africa*, African Studies Centre: Leiden.

Kosheleva, S & Zavyalova, E 2011, *Gender Aspects of Human Resource Development in Contemporary Russia*, Saint Petersburg State University: Saint Petersburg.

OECD 2012, *Human Resource Management Country Profile, OECD*.

Onday, O 2016, Human Resource Theory, *Global Journal of Human resource Management*, vol. 4, no.1, pp. 95-110.

Senyucel, Z 2009, *Managing Human Resource in the 21st Century*, London Business School: London.

Shen, J, Chanda, A, D'Netto, B & Monga, M 2009, Managing Diversity through Human Resource Management, *The International Journal of Human Resource Management*, vol. 20, no. 2, pp. 235-251.

Standing, H 1999, Gender- a Missing Dimension in Human Resource Policy and Planning for Health Reforms, *Special Article*.

YOUR KNOWLEDGE HAS VALUE

- We will publish your bachelor's and master's thesis, essays and papers

- Your own eBook and book - sold worldwide in all relevant shops

- Earn money with each sale

Upload your text at www.GRIN.com and publish for free